Setting Captives Free

95
Theses
for
Pure Reformation

Mike Cleveland

Setting Captives Free
95 Theses for Pure Reformation
by Mike Cleveland

Inquiries should be addressed to
Focus Publishing
Rights and Permissions Dept.
PO Box 665
Bemidji, Minnesota 56619

Cover Design by Gayle Yarrington

ISBN: 1-885904-40-1

Printed in the United States of America

95
Theses
for
Pure Reformation

Table of Contents

The Problem

The Solution for the Captive

The Solution for the Spouse

Solutions for Church Leadership

Introduction

In my years of bondage to sin I was filled with impurity in my heart, and without the grace of Jesus Christ I would yet be enslaved to my impulses and a captive to lust. My hypocrisy was that I pretended to be a leader in the Christian community while I lived the double life of a porn-slave. Therefore, I have compassion for those who are in the iron chains of bondage, including those in leadership who struggle with impurity.

Those of us who have been redeemed from captivity to sexual impurity have a strong desire to see others set free by the power of the gospel. We have no place to throw stones or judge the hearts of others, recognizing our own depravity apart from grace.

Pornography and masturbation (referred to as "P and M" from here on) are at epidemic proportions in the church of Jesus Christ today, and the church needs to know how to combat it. The source of the epidemic is:

> **The World's Message:** This world thinks nothing of displaying impurity in all of it's media sources. The message of this world is that sexual impurity is normal, natural, fun, enjoyable, and harmless. We are bombarded daily by this message from many sources. With the invention of the internet this message has become a loud shout that demands to be heard.
>
> **The Flesh's Message:** The flesh has always demanded gratification. The flesh communicates to us that it must be satisfied, it must be allowed to experience pleasure, and that it can not be denied. The flesh listens to the message of the world and heartily agrees and requires us to listen.
>
> **The Devil's Message:** The enemy of our souls is behind this epidemic of P and M and all forms of sexual impurity. This point needs to be understood by the church in order to combat it effectively.

These theses are offered to the church to call men and women away from

1

dining with the devil and call them instead to a feast at the table of the King. They are designed to be a forthright wake up call for the church to repent of the intoxication of pornography and sexual impurity, and to teach the repentant to discover the love of Jesus Christ which is "better than wine." This is an earnest plea to the pastors of God's Church to shepherd God's flock both in the integrity of their own hearts and the skillfulness of their hands, in helping others to freedom. Leaders who are strong in purity are bold and powerful in protecting their flock against the evil one, but leaders who are weak in purity produce a flock of lambs that are easy prey.

Note: The references to those involved in impurity are in the masculine (he, him, his) for the sake of brevity. However, we do recognize that P and M are increasingly a problem with both genders.

The
Problem

The Problem

1. P and M blinds the mind to the gospel (2 Corinthians 4:3-4) and darkens the understanding (Ephesians 4:18).

The one trapped in sexual idolatry does not see God properly; therefore he does not perceive spiritual truth accurately. His view of God is warped, his theology is distorted, and true understanding of the gospel is veiled. Church leadership should help the captive to understand his skewed condition, and bring before him the true character of God, asking him to turn to the Lord and forsake his sin and his false perceptions (2 Corinthians 3:16-17). Leadership should also refuse to allow any who are under the hypnotic power of pornography, masturbation, or sexual impurity to teach God's Word in any capacity (Romans 2:21-22). Their clouded view of God and their distorted reasoning will impact those they teach and the result will be that others are infected by their false views. Purity precedes perception (Matthew 5:8). Those who teach should have a pure heart, a good conscience and sincere faith, so that "strange doctrines" are not taught (1 Timothy 1:3-5).

If the captive has been around church for awhile or is schooled in theology he may have knowledge, but he does not have the "light of the knowledge of the glory of Jesus Christ" (2 Corinthians 4:6). Knowledge does not equate to righteousness even as information is not the same as transformation. An enlightened mind and a strong character are the results of purity of heart. Leadership must not be duped by one who is greatly knowledgeable in Scripture, and they must help the captive to understand that strength of character and light in understanding are more important than knowledge. Those in impurity can be quite articulate in the Scriptures, but the Kingdom of God is not a matter of talk, but of power (1 Corinthians 4:19-20).

2. P and M consume the imagination (Genesis 6:5) and set up thought-strongholds (2 Corinthians 10:3-5).

Those who give themselves over to the secret sins of P and M live their lives with their minds fixed on sexual escapades with others. Everyone with whom they come in contact becomes an object of fantasy to stimulate sexual scenarios. Their imaginations are the devil's playground. Leadership must require the captive to "radically amputate" (Matthew 5:29-30) all access to pornography and hold them accountable to maintaining zero access (Romans 13:14) (this will no doubt require creativity), helping them to understand that the fire of sinful lust will eventually die out when starved of fuel (Proverbs 26:20). Once radical amputation is in place leadership needs to teach the captive how to replace his fantasizing with thoughts that are true, honorable, right and pure (Philippians 4:8).

3. P and M make a man double-minded and unstable in all his ways (Psalm 119:113; James 1:8; Proverbs 5:6; 2 Peter 2:14).

A sin captive is hypocritical and duplistic, requiring much from those around him but failing to live up to his own standards. He is described aptly in Psalm 12:2, "with a double heart they speak." He wavers between two opinions (his conscience convicts him but he loves his sin). He draws near to God with his mouth, and honors him with his lips, but his heart is far from God (Matthew 15:8). This duplicity of mind and heart make the man unstable in all his ways, confused in his mind and restless in his thoughts. Leadership should consider the man's "ways" more than listening to his words. There is a great need to provide a sin-captive with the hope that if he is freed by grace from the trap of impurity his thoughts will become singular (Psalm 27:4; Ecclesiastes 7:18) and his life will become stable (Colossians 2:5). Isaiah 26:3 says, "The steadfast of mind Thou wilt will keep in perfect peace, Because he trusts in Thee."

4. P and M deceive the heart (Titus 3:3) and enslave the captive (Romans 6:16; 2 Peter 2:19).

Those who sin in this manner believe lies of the devil as they eat the fruit he gives them. They are described in Isaiah 44:20. "He feeds on ashes; a deceived heart has turned him aside. And he cannot deliver himself, nor say, 'Is there not a lie in my right hand?'" His heart is "deceived," and he cannot deliver himself because he is enslaved. Church leadership should understand that in dealing with slaves to impurity they will hear many lies, and that to effectively help the captive to freedom they must challenge those lies and help the captive to replace them with the truth (John 8:32).

6

5. P and M become the god of the one who is deceived and enslaved (Colossians 3:5).

He begins to worship the enticing images and the exhilarating experience he has while sinning. He turns to this god whenever he is bored or lonely, tired or stressed, when he needs comfort or for sexual intimacy. He adulterates his heart before this god, longs to worship this god at all times, and gives his heart to his god both before and during the worship experience. The devil has always desired the worship of God's children: "...and he (the devil) said to Him, 'All these things I will give You, if You fall down and worship me'" (Matthew 4:9). P and M is one way the devil is seducing God's children to worship him.

6. P and M are idolatrous (Colossians 3:5) and therefore demonic (1 Corinthians 10:20).

The church must recognize that members who sin in this manner are bowing down to a demonic shrine, though they profess to worship the true and living God. They are giving the devil a foothold in their lives (Ephesians 4:27). Since these sins are normally committed in the dark (Job 24:15) leadership should humbly seek out those who are in bondage and develop a plan for their release from captivity (Galatians 6:1). In light of the seriousness of these sins, it is unacceptable to allow a member of the church that falls habitually in this area to go on in his sin without discipline. Most porn slaves who attend church will fall every 2-4 weeks on average, but some can go 2 months or longer before they must gratify their flesh again. It is unloving to allow the sin that dishonors Christ, defiles the church, and destroys the home to go undisciplined.

7. P and M defile the conscience (Titus 1:15; 1 Timothy 1:19), harden the heart (Hebrews 3:13) and corrupt the soul (Job 15:16; Ezekiel 23:11; 2 Peter 2:10).

When we say that someone is "struggling with impurity" what is really true is that he is defiling his conscience, hardening his heart and corrupting his soul every time he falls. The effects of this defilement, hardening and corruption are spread to all with whom the captive comes in contact, in one way or another (Romans 5:12; 2 Timothy 2:17). Leadership must understand the true condition of the captive (defiled, hardened and corrupted) and be earnest in helping him to freedom, persistent in checking on his condition, and must be

7

unified and relentless in their activity of graciously and humbly helping him escape the trap he is in (2 Timothy 2:25-26).

8. P and M lead to living a life of deception.

The one in bondage to impurity hides his sin in order to protect himself from being discovered. He thinks nobody sees his secret sinning. "The eye of the adulterer waits for the twilight, Saying, 'No eye will see me.' And he disguises his face" (Job 24:15). This hiding, secrecy and deception begins to characterize his life (2 Timothy 3:13) and after some time in this bondage he has been transformed into a habitual liar who runs to his lies for shelter. "For we have made falsehood our refuge and we have concealed ourselves with deception" (Isaiah 28:15). "They conceive mischief and bring forth iniquity, and their mind prepares deception" (Job 15:35).

9. P and M damage and eventually destroy the relationship with God.

"He who turns away his ear from listening to the law, even his prayer is an abomination" (Proverbs 28:9). Those who practice P and M within the church are in danger of losing all relationship with God because they are serving the master of impurity and because of their worship of demons. These theses are not meant to be a study on the subject of eternal security, but rather to warn those who practice the idolatry of sexual impurity (Colossians 3:5) that they are in danger of losing any relationship with God that they have claimed to have (1 Corinthians 6:9-10). It is impossible to serve two masters, either we will love the one and hate the other or we will serve the one and despise the other (Matthew 6:24).

10. P and M damage and can destroy marital relationships.

P and M are extremely selfish activities that become unbreakable habits (John 8:34), and habits of selfishness in marriage damage the marital relationship, sometimes beyond repair. P and M is heart adultery (Matthew 5:28) and because a man eventually becomes outwardly what he is inwardly (Proverbs 23:7), it often leads to physical adultery. Physical adultery and sexual impurity break the marriage vow and are often followed by separation, divorce and the ruin of the family. The devil comes to kill, steal and destroy (John 10:10), and this includes marriages and families.

11. P and M damage and can ruin sexual intimacy and brings the judgment of God.

Partaking in the demonic activities of P and M are extremely degrading to the spouse of the pornographer. The spouse becomes the first target for the sexual perversion that P and M encourage. The spouse feels that he or she is simply the target for the gratification of the lusts of the one who is being duped by the devil, and it depersonalizes and dehumanizes the spouse. This can lead to the spouse denying sex to the captive, which can then prompt the captive to turn further to P and M, and the cycle becomes a destructive force to the marriage. Because the captive has become a heart adulterer through P and M, he has defiled his marriage, and defilement is that which ruins intimacy. Unless he repents the adulterer not only ruins sexual intimacy in marriage but he is also in danger of the judgment of God. "Let marriage be held in honor among all, and let the marriage bed be undefiled; for fornicators and adulterers God will judge" (Hebrews 13:4).

12. P and M damage and can destroy relationships within the family.

The captive to impurity is fixated on gratifying his lusts (Ephesians 2:3), and this goal begins to consume him, often to the neglect of his family. This selfishness on the part of the captive has the potential to permanently destroy relationships in his family. Also, the captive brings impurity into the family (whether he recognizes it or not), and impurity defiles his spouse and his children. Often as a result of the captive bringing impurity into his family, the spouse will become bitter which also defiles many. So the home becomes an environment where impurity and bitterness thrive.

The nature of lust is to drag captives away from all that is good and right, including their families. "But each one is tempted when he is carried away and enticed by his own lust" (James 1:14). The next step after the captive is carried away is often the death of family relationships. "Then when lust has conceived, it gives birth to sin; and when sin is accomplished, it brings forth death" (James 1:15).

13. P and M damage and can destroy relationships within the church (2 Corinthians 6:14).

1 John 1:7 says, "but if we walk in the light as He Himself is in the light, we have fellowship with one another, and the blood of Jesus His Son cleanses us

9

from all sin." Walking in the light is a prerequisite for fellowship among Christians. Those who are involved in the darkness of secret sin lose their ability to interact with each other in a gracious, kind and caring manner as their secret sins make them prideful, irritable and self-conscious (Jude 1:16). Like Adam after he sinned, they are hiding and not wanting to be found out (John 3:20), they try to cover themselves to prevent discovery, and they are quick to shift blame to others. It is this covering and self-protection which ruins open and intimate fellowship among believers. Church growth is stymied when impurity thrives. Leadership needs to help the captive understand that the reason he is at odds with others is most likely because he is not walking in the light (1 Timothy 6:5), and to assure him that as he makes full disclosure of and repents of sin fellowship will be restored.

14. P and M mar the witness and ruin the testimony of a Christian (Colossians 4:5; Titus 2:9-10).

Christians are to be the light of the world but if we live in darkness we lose our testimony. Many captives are able to articulate the Scriptures while they are in bondage, and they think by their words that people will come to a saving knowledge of Christ. This may indeed happen, but if so it is because God has blinded the seeker to the destructive force of impurity within the professing believer, and has opened his ears to hear the message of the gospel, despite the defiled messenger it comes through.

15. P and M damage and can destroy ministries.

God has ordained that people would be saved through the preaching of the gospel, but gospel preaching from a sin-captive lacks spiritual authority. It is the minister who will cleanse himself from all impurity that will discover his usefulness in ministry. "Therefore, if a man cleanses himself from these things, he will be a vessel for honor, sanctified, useful to the Master, prepared for every good work. Now flee from youthful lusts and pursue righteousness, faith, love and peace, with those who call on the Lord from a pure heart" (2 Timothy 2:21-22). "In this case, moreover, it is required of stewards that one be found trustworthy" (1 Corinthians 4:2).

16. P and M drain the resources of the captive.

His time, energy, and money all dwindle as he gives himself over to the pursuit of impurity. "You have sown much, but harvest little; you eat, but there is not enough to be satisfied; you drink, but there is not enough to become drunk;

you put on clothing, but no one is warm enough; and he who earns, earns wages to put into a purse with holes. Thus says the LORD of hosts, 'Consider your ways!'" (Haggai 1:6-7).

Any who give themselves to lust experience loss. Following cravings eventually leads to wasting time, money, talents, assets, creativity, productivity, etc. "But (they) craved intensely in the wilderness, and tempted God in the desert. So He gave them their request, but sent a wasting disease among them" (Psalm 106:14-15).

17. P and M limit the development and stunt the growth of the captive.

Growth in the Christian life comes from many things, one of which is drinking the pure milk of the Word of God (1 Peter 2:2). Since those who are captive to P and M are "feeding on ashes" (Isaiah 44:20) and attempting to quench their thirst by drinking from a "broken cistern" (Jeremiah 2:13), their souls are parched and dehydrated. They are "failing to thrive" and their spiritual growth is stunted because they are not truly drinking in the Word of God, despite the fact that they may be reading, studying and memorizing it.

18. P and M may lead to socio-pathic depravity.

Ted Bundy is one story among many who have ended up socially depraved because of their bondage to impurity. Scripture teaches us that those involved in deception go from bad to worse (2 Timothy 3:13), and many are those who would have been repulsed in the early stages about what they now view on a regular basis. Obviously not all who are captive to lust become murderers. The point is that there is the potential for anyone to become socially depraved if they habitually pursue their lusts.

> "Ephraim was a watchman with my God, a prophet; yet the snare of a bird catcher is in all his ways, and there is only hostility in the house of his God. They have gone deep in depravity...they came to Baal-peor and devoted themselves to shame, and they became as detestable as that which they loved" (Hosea 9:8-10).

> "And just as they did not see fit to acknowledge God any longer, God gave them over to a depraved mind, to do those things which are not proper" (Romans 1:28).

19. P and M obscures the glory of God in the captive.

The glory of God in the life of any Christian is obscured by sin. Once habitual sin is removed by grace, the captive begins to bring honor and glory to God as He evidences contentment in the Lord. The Christian's main duty is to glorify God (1 Corinthians 6:20) and enjoy Him forever. Sin prevents the enjoyment of God, thus obscuring the glory of God in the captive.

20. P and M destroy and can result in death.

Impurity destroys a man's relationship with God (Isaiah 1:15; 1 Corinthians 6:9). Sexual immorality cherished in the heart and/or acted on in the life destroys marriages (Matthew 5:32). Sinful lust allowed to continue in a church will destroy the church, even as sexual immorality destroys society (Genesis 19; Jude 1:7). However, simply telling a pornography addict that his ways lead to death will not help him find life or escape his sinful trap. Leadership must help the captive see that apart from breaking the cycle of sin, death covers the soul (James 1:13-16). If he truly has the Son he will truly have life (1 John 5:12), but leadership might need to warn the heart-adulterer that it is possible to be deceived about his eternal destiny (1 Corinthians 6:9) and that he may thus be destroyed.

The
Solution
for the
Captive

The Solution for the Captive

21. The Cross and The Gospel of God's Grace

There is no hope for freedom from sin apart from the gospel. There are no man-made methods or psychological techniques that can unshackle us. Only God's grace is stronger than the pull of sin. The gospel says that God placed our sins on His own Son, that He then radically amputated His Son (Isaiah 53: 8) on the cross, thereby forgiving our sins, canceling our debt, and doing away with our sin forever. Because our sins were placed on Jesus and because He paid the price for them (separation from God and death) (Romans 6:23), God can be just in forgiving our sins (Romans 3:26), removing our guilt and shame (Leviticus 26:13), and giving us a new life (Acts 5:20). We are not able to set ourselves free from sin by trying hard. We cannot muster up faith and repentance, nor can we escape the trap of the devil by our own efforts. But by God's grace, through the forgiveness of the cross, we can be freed of sin's guilt (Isaiah 53:10), sin's curse (Galatians 3:13), and sin's power (Romans 6:14). Freedom from sin comes by God's grace (Titus 2:11-12) and nothing else.

> "For while we were still helpless, at the right time
> Christ died for the ungodly" (Romans 5:6).

> "For I delivered to you as of first importance what I
> also received, that Christ died for our sins according
> to the Scriptures, and that He was buried, and that
> He was raised on the third day according to the Scrip-
> tures" (I Corinthians 15:3-4).

22. Brokenness

As we see the love of God in Jesus Christ, as He bears our sin burden and suffers on the cross in our place, we begin to experience heart pain for the pain our sins brought to the heart of God. We become brokenhearted and the reality of our years of sinful bondage begins to crush us. As we look to the cross we see such love demonstrated toward us, and we feel so unworthy that we are the recipients of God's love and grace, that we are further broken and humbled. "The sacrifices of God are a broken spirit; a broken and a contrite heart, O God, You will not despise" (Psalm 51:17).

15

This lowly, broken and humbled condition is where God must take us if we want to be freed from sin. The man who thinks himself whole and healthy and has a good opinion of himself is not yet ready to be free from sin (Luke 5:32). Freedom comes through the breaking down of our pride, the crushing of our spirit, and ruining of our estimation of ourselves. "The Lord is near to the brokenhearted and saves those who are crushed in spirit" (Psalm 34:18). We must be crushed, wounded, bruised and killed before we can be made alive and healed (Hosea 6:1-3). Embrace the brokenness that comes by God's grace, for it has a good end result.

> "Then I went down to the potter's house, and there he was, making something on the wheel. But the vessel that he was making of clay was spoiled in the hand of the potter; so he remade it into another vessel, as it pleased the potter to make. Then the word of the LORD came to me saying, 'Can I not, O house of Israel, deal with you as this potter does?' declares the LORD. 'Behold, like the clay in the potter's hand, so are you in My hand, O house of Israel'" (Jeremiah 18:3-6).

23. Confession to God

When we become broken in heart and crushed in spirit, because of our sin and because of God's grace, we need to confess our sins. Sin is primarily against God and one of the first steps we must take is to make an open and honest confession of sin to God. "So it shall be when he becomes guilty in one of these, that he shall confess that in which he has sinned" (Leviticus 5:5). "If we confess our sins, He is faithful and just to forgive us our sins and cleanse us from all unrighteousness" (1 John 1:9). Confessing our sins to God is simply agreeing with God that what we have been and what we have done has been wrong, and that we are sorry for our sins.

As we are confessing to the Lord, it helps to give our sins biblical titles, such as "Lord I ask forgiveness for committing the sin of heart adultery in viewing pornography and for gratifying the lusts of my flesh through masturbation." Or, "I confess to You my sexual impurity, which has made me an idolater, and I ask your forgiveness."

24. Repentance

Sexual impurity has one root cause, and many contributing factors. The root cause is a heart problem (Matthew 15:18-20), the contributing factors can be a sinful family upbringing, early exposure to pornography or sexual abuse, lack of emotional intimacy, etc... Sexual impurity is idolatry (Colossians 3:5) and freedom comes only as we recognize it as such, lay aside our excuses, turn from our sin and begin serving the Lord (1 Thessalonians 1:9). Repentance is far more than "feeling badly that I sinned". It is experiencing godly sorrow and then turning away from sin and to the Lord. Psychological remedies (snapping the wrist with a rubber band when tempted, visualizing an emotional experience when tempted, etc...) are wholly insufficient to change the heart, to grant repentance, or to produce lasting freedom. God alone can change the heart (John 12:40) and grant repentance to us who have been captive to sin (2 Timothy 2:25-26). He replaces the sinful desires with life-giving ones (Psalm 119:45).

Repentance is a gift of God (2 Timothy 2:25-26) and comes by His grace. Therefore we must seek after and find the grace of God in Jesus Christ (Matthew 7:7-11) in order to enjoy lasting freedom. The receiving of this grace will enable genuine repentance and will then teach us, as freed captives to say no to ungodliness and to live sensibly, righteously and godly (Titus 2:11-12).

25. Confession of Sin to Others

Godly sorrow in the heart leads to turning away from sin. This godly sorrow is directed toward God (Psalm 51:4) and we who want to find freedom must confess our sins to the Lord (1 John 1:8-9). Then, if we are repentant we will want to confess sins to any person we have sinned against. Sin is like a fungus, it grows best in the dark. But if we turn the light on it eventually it withers and dies (Ephesians 5:11-14). Confessing to others is turning the light on our sin. This confession might best be done in the presence of our pastor. The confession should not minimize sin ("I'm sorry I had a small affair"), but rather should be stated in biblical terms: "I ask your forgiveness for committing adultery," or "my ongoing masturbation has stolen intimacy from us; will you forgive me?"

Nobody will sustain lasting freedom who hides sin, and compassion and grace are given as we humble ourselves and make confession. Proverbs 28:13 says, "He who conceals his transgressions will not prosper, but he who confesses and forsakes them will find compassion." It is not enough to confess our sins to God alone, we must also confess to those we sin against. Confession of sin brings with it a healing power, which is one of the reasons why the devil plants many plausible thoughts in our minds to keep us from confessing to others. James 5:16 says, "Therefore, confess your sins to one another, and pray for one another so that you may be healed. The effective prayer of a righteous man can accomplish much."

26. Radical Amputation

The manner of being free from sinful lust is to radically amputate every avenue through which it enters, and to be radical in cutting it off at the source: "If your right eye makes you stumble, tear it out and throw it from you; for it is better for you that one of the parts of your body perish, than for your whole body to go into hell. And if your right hand makes you stumble, cut it off and throw it from you; for it is better for you that one of the parts of your body perish, than for your whole body to go into hell" (Matthew 5:29,30).

Jesus is not teaching here the dismembering of our bodies. Rather he is teaching the need to be radical in cutting out those avenues through which sin enters. In other words, He is saying to make it so that it is practically impossible to view pornography (get rid of the source of temptation) or to gratify our flesh in masturbation. (We know that "plucking out the eye" and "cutting off the hand" are symbolic expressions, since they come in the midst of a sermon about the heart.) We who truly want victory will not allow any provision for our flesh, to gratify the lusts thereof (Romans 13:14), for we recognize that if it is available we might turn to it in a weak moment. God the Father dealt with sin in this radical manner. Jesus was "cut off" from the land of the living after God placed our sins on Him (Isaiah 53:8).

The story of Achan in Joshua 7 teaches that hidden defilement weakens the ability to fight. Only as the Israelites "radically amputated" Achan and his entire family did they have victory over their enemies. Purity precedes power.

This does not mean that radical amputation is the entire answer to overcoming sin. It is an important step in the change process, but it is not the whole process itself. This step can't be overlooked, but it must be accompanied with ongoing seeking of the Lord and growth in grace if we really want to be free.

If you want to be free consider every avenue through which you have fallen, and set out to make it so that you have zero access to it in the future. The devil lies and says that real victory would be to have the way to gratify ourselves and refuse it. There does come a time when this victory can indeed happen, but initially the way to freedom is through a radical removal of the source of temptation: "Pluck out the eye," "cut off the hand". As we are radical in amputation we find freedom (Proverbs 23:1).

27. Radical Appropriation

If we cut off access to all pornography and refuse to masturbate, we will now have a void (Luke 11:24-26). We used to turn to pornography and masturbation as a drunkard turns to alcohol: for excitement, stress relief, comfort, medicating of pain, etc... Now, because of radical amputation this option is not available and we must learn to replace this previous sinful energy in pursuing our idolatry with pursuing the Lord (1 Timothy 6:11). We have previously been "feeding on ashes" (Isaiah 44:20) and our souls are starved for nutrition. Now, as we cut off all our ability to feed on that which destroys the soul it becomes important to begin learning how to truly feed on Jesus (John 6:50-58).

28. Radical Accountability

We who have indulged in the sin of impurity have made sure that our lives are private so that nobody will discover our sin, and we have been accountable to no one. Now, when we seek to be free we need to learn how to invite accountability into our lives, as daily encouragement is an antidote to the power of sin: "But encourage one another day after day, as long as it is still called 'Today,' lest any one of you be hardened by the deceitfulness of sin" (Hebrews 3:13).

Accountability does not mean a support group, though accountability can happen there. It means reporting in to someone as to how I am living, how my walk with the Lord is, how my sin struggles are going. As our indulging in sin was daily, so now accountability needs to be daily as well (Hebrews 3:13).

29. Ongoing Humility

Just as pride goes before a fall, humility and freedom from sin go hand in hand with one another (Proverbs 16:18). When a person will implement radical amputation, radical appropriation and radical accountability, they will indeed get free from habitual sin, but then pride becomes a temptation. The way to avoid the trap of pride is to consciously live in the presence of God, for no man can remain in pride when in God's presence (Isaiah 6:1-5). "Humble yourselves in the presence of the Lord, and He will exalt you" (James 4:10). We need to seek to learn, to grow, ask questions, and seek help from others. These will keep us humble.

30. Hunger For Truth

True humility should be evidenced by a hunger for the truth. "He humbled you and let you be hungry, and fed you with manna which you did not know, nor did your fathers know, that He might make you understand that man does not live by bread alone, but man lives by everything that proceeds out of the mouth of the LORD" (Deuteronomy 8:3). Simultaneous to God working in our hearts to free us from sin we begin to crave His Word (1 Peter 2:2). As righteousness is a cool drink and real food to the soul, we begin hungering and thirsting for it, and we notice we are becoming satisfied in it (Matthew 5:6). Our souls now feed on truth rather than on deception and we learn to maintain this hunger for truth.

31. Identity In Christ

Who we see ourselves to be influences our actions. As Christians we have been crucified with Christ and we no longer live, the old has gone, the new has come (Galatians 2:20). Our old man is dead and buried and in salvation we have a new nature and a new life. That is our identity. The problem with sin struggles come in because our new man lives in flesh, and our flesh is not redeemed (Romans 8:23). But the fact that we still have flesh is no excuse to sin. "Even so, consider yourselves to be dead to sin, but alive to God in Christ Jesus" (Romans 6:11).

We are not teaching "sinless perfection" because, as mentioned above, we still have weak flesh and a powerful enemy, but we are teaching that our identity is in our new man who was created in true holiness and righteousness (Ephesians 4:24).

> "The one who practices sin is of the devil; for the devil has sinned from the beginning. The Son of God appeared for this purpose, that He might destroy the works of the devil. No one who is born of God practices sin, because His seed abides in him; and he cannot sin, because he is born of God. By this the children of God and the children of the devil are obvious; anyone who does not practice righteousness is

not of God, nor the one who does not love his brother"
(1 John 3:8-10).

Our identity in Christ is important to see. Christians do not have two natures, or salvation would be addition (a good nature added to our bad nature when we're saved). Salvation is not addition, but rather transformation. Our old man was put to death, we no longer have an old nature, but rather we are only new creations in Christ and this needs to be our identity.

32. Exclusive Drinking

John Piper says that God is most glorified in us when we are most satisfied in Him. Those who are redeemed learn to say, "All my springs of joy are in You" (Psalm 87:7), and Paul said, "For me to live is Christ" (Philippians 1:21). All of these authors are saying the same thing. Christians are those who learn to find their sole source of joy, refreshment, and life in Jesus Christ. This does not mean that we can't have hobbies or enjoy our families, etc... It simply means that we learn how to enjoy the Lord in it all. The one who will "drink" exclusively from the fountain of joy in Jesus will have eternal pleasure (Psalm 16:11) and is in no danger of falling to habitual sin. "The joy of the Lord is my strength" (Nehemiah 8:10).

33. Demolishing Strongholds

P and M become thought strongholds that the captive is unable to shake. These thought-strongholds are demonic and they require divine power to demolish. Spiritual warfare is about depending upon God's power to demolish demonic strongholds. We are not able to simply rid our minds of these thoughts. In order to be free from them we must experience the power of God that enables us to take our thoughts captives to Jesus Christ. Depending upon the power of God brings victory and we can be free from these dominating thoughts.

> "For though we walk in the flesh, we do not war according to the flesh, for the weapons of our warfare are not of the flesh, but divinely powerful for the destruction of fortresses. We are destroying speculations and every lofty thing raised up against the knowledge of God, and we are taking every thought captive to the obedience of Christ" (2 Corinthians 10:3-5).

34. Breaking The Chain

There is usually a chain of events that leads up to self-indulgence. In Genesis 13 Lot "saw" the well watered plain of the Jordan (verse 10), then he "set out towards" it (verse 11), then he "pitched his tent near" it (verse 12), next he was "living in it" (Genesis 14:12) and finally he was "taken captive" (Genesis 14:12) by the raiding army and became a prisoner. The captive to P and M must learn to "break the chain" by noticing what events lead up to our captivity, and removing a link in the accident chain.

35. Claiming God's Promises

"...seeing that His divine power has granted to us everything pertaining to life and godliness, through the true knowledge of Him who called us by His own glory and excellence. For by these He has granted to us His precious and magnificent promises, in order that by them you may become partakers of the divine nature, having escaped the corruption that is in the world by lust" (2 Peter 1:3-4).

Notice that it is by the promises of God that we escape corruption. We whose souls have been corrupted by impurity and lust must learn to receive and act upon the promises found in God's Word which will bring freedom from corruption. "Sanctify them in the truth; Thy word is truth" (John 17:17).

36. Walking in the Light

Sin thrives in darkness: "For everyone who does evil hates the light, and does not come to the light, lest his deeds should be exposed" (John 3:20). We will have victory over it as we drag it into the light. "But he who practices truth comes to the light that his deeds may be manifested as having been wrought in God" (John 3:21). Like a fungus, sin that is exposed to the light soon withers and dies as mercy is granted to us. Proverbs 28:13 says: "He who conceals his transgressions will not prosper, but he who confesses and forsakes them will find compassion."

We who desire freedom from P and M should not say: "I have confessed my sins to God and that is sufficient". Sadly, the power of darkness still resides within hearts that believe this. The joy of true, everlasting freedom will not come if we believe this way. Why? Because we have not humbled ourselves before our fellow man! "If we say that we have fellowship with Him and yet walk in darkness, we lie and do not practice the truth. But if we walk in the light, as He Himself is in the light, we have fellowship with one another, and the blood of Jesus His Son cleanses us from all sin" (1 John 1:6-7).

When we confess our sins to fellow Christians there is an evidencing of humility. Matthew 23:12 says, "And whoever exalts himself shall be humbled, and whoever humbles himself shall be exalted."

For the soul freed from the chains of darkness, there is a great desire to continue walking in the light of this new found liberty, and to live their lives with their hearts as 'open books' for others to see what is written within. "It was for freedom that Christ set us free; therefore keep standing firm and do not be subject again to a yoke of slavery" (Galatians 5:1).

37. Growing in Grace

True life begins when God births us into His kingdom by grace (1 Peter 1:23) and then the Christian life is one of growing from a little child, to a young man, to a father (1 John 2:12-14). Sin is that which stunts the growth and hinders the spiritual development of a Christian. Pornography and masturbation can come into the life of a Christian (Galatians 6:1) but because of the selfish and unloving nature of habitual sin it will stifle spiritual growth and cause immaturity (1 Corinthians 13:11). Sexual impurity is very selfish and childish, and part of becoming free from its grip is to grow in grace. Growing in grace happens as we repent of the deceit of impurity and begin drinking in the Word of God. "Therefore, putting aside all malice and all guile and hypocrisy and envy and all slander, like newborn babes, long for the pure milk of the word, that by it you may grow in respect to salvation" (1 Peter 2:1-2).

For 15 years I was in all kinds of sexual impurity, while a professing Christian. I was stunted in growth, immature, despite having knowledge. If you are likewise involved in pornography, masturbation or other forms of sexual impurity I urge you to radically amputate ("laying aside all deceit"), radically appropriate ("long for the pure milk of the word") and be radically accountable (Hebrews 3:13). Growth will come, and along with it, maturity and stability.

38. Submission to Spiritual Authority

A key element to finding freedom is to not only go to church but to willingly place ourselves under the leadership of the church. We are not only to hear God's Word from our pastor/elders but we are also to submit to their authority in our lives. God designed the shepherds (pastor/elders) to protect the sheep from the evil one (Acts 20:28) and ongoing freedom requires our submission to them. Indeed, we have not seen lasting freedom come into any life that refuses to find and submit to a spiritual authority who can assume responsibility for his soul.

> "Obey your leaders and submit to them, for they keep watch over your souls as those who will give an account. Let them do this with joy and not with grief, for this would be unprofitable for you" (Hebrews13:17).

39. Follow Godly Leaders

Not only do we need to find and submit ourselves to the authority of the church but we also need to look for godly men within the church and imitate and follow them. By godly men we mean those that have a heart for the Lord, compassion for His people and are disciplined in their lifestyle. "For you yourselves know how you ought to follow our example, because we did not act in an undisciplined manner among you" (2 Thessalonians 3:7).

> "Remember those who led you, who spoke the word of God to you; and considering the result of their conduct, imitate their faith" (Hebrews 13:7).

40. Restore the Marriage Relationship

We who have been involved in sexual impurity (pornography, masturbation, adultery, or any other form of impurity) have broken the trust of our spouses. Two things need to happen in order for the relationship to be restored and to become healthy: Forgiveness and trust. Forgiveness should happen instantly, upon confession (Luke 17:4), but trust takes time to restore, and should grow in direct proportion to the fruit of repentance in the life of the one seeking to restore the relationship.

In order to redevelop trust with our spouses we need to be willing to have our lives be an open book to them. Since we are "one" with our spouses there should be no secrecy, no separate accounts, no separate lives. Restoring the marriage relationship will no doubt take time, effort and much prayer. Hearts have been hurt, our spouses have felt betrayed, belittled and ignored, and it will no doubt require much patience and willingness on our parts to restore the areas that our sin tore down.

We should be willing to have our spouses check the history on our computer, review all charges on our credit cards, ask us about long distance phone calls, know where we are and whom we are with at any time during the day or night, and have full and complete access to our lives. Independence is not acceptable in a Christian marriage, but rather interdependence is God's design (1 Corinthians 11:8-12).

41. Restore Sexual Intimacy

P and M provide an intimacy, but it is a false intimacy because it takes two to enjoy real intimacy. Intimacy is more than just sexual intercourse, it is the sharing of two lives, walking with one another through the peaks and valleys, and the promise to remain committed to each other, forsaking all others, for life. We who have given ourselves over to the false intimacy must now learn how to enjoy true intimacy in marriage.

Sexual intimacy in marriage is a very powerful deterrent to the devil's operation in our lives, and if we want to enjoy victory over impurity we must focus on maintaining an active sex life with our spouses. "Stop depriving one another, except by agreement for a time, that you may devote yourselves to prayer, and come together again lest Satan tempt you because of your lack of self-control" (1 Corinthians 7:5). This verse tells us that if we deprive one another of sexual intimacy, except for a mutually agreed upon time to seek the Lord, we are opening the door to the devil. This is a very serious error to make in a marriage. Seek to do whatever it takes to make your love life thrive at home, including the total forsaking of all forms of impurity, and the cultivating of love in the marriage. Learn to enjoy sexual intimacy with your spouse as the only outlet for sexual desire.

Impurity always breaks sexual intimacy. It defiles the marriage bed and ruins true love and sexual oneness. Usually restoring this area begins with small steps in the right direction, yet there is an urgency to restore this part of the relationship so that the devil will not split apart the marriage.

"The wife does not have authority over her own body, but the husband does; and likewise also the husband does not have authority over his own body, but the wife does." (1 Corinthians 7:4).

42. Restore Family Relationships

The captive to impurity has shown that nothing is as important as gratifying his lusts, including his family. Now, in repentance, his heart is being turned back toward his family. We who have been in bondage and have hurt our children need to regain their trust by evidencing our repentance in many ways to them. They have sensed that there is something wrong with us and in some cases we may have even exposed them to our impurity. We must now set out to show them that we are no longer idolatrous but that we love God and our families.

> "It is he who will go as a forerunner before Him in the spirit and power of Elijah, TO TURN THE HEARTS OF THE FATHERS BACK TO THE CHILDREN, and the disobedient to the attitude of the righteous, so as to make ready a people prepared for the Lord" (Luke 1:17).

43. Reestablish Fellowship in the Church

Captivity to P and M make a man irritable, edgy, easily angered, self-protective, and prideful. These attitudes of the heart drive people away and cause rifts in the church. When we are granted repentance we can begin to restore these relationships in the church by evidencing humility, becoming quiet and teachable, and evidencing willingness to yield and a desire to be at peace with all, as far as is possible.

> "But the wisdom which is from heaven is first holy, then gentle, readily giving way in argument, full of peace and mercy and good works, not doubting, not seeming other than it is" (James 3:17, Bible in Basic English).

44. Servanthood

We previously lived to gratify our flesh and it was a very selfish existence (Ephesians 2:2-3). But now part of freedom includes turning from ourselves to serve others instead of ourselves (John 13:14-17). Seeking to be a vessel useful to the Master is one of the best ways that we can protect ourselves from falling in the future, for serving others is the opposite of what we did in our selfish lives of pornographic addiction. We have been chosen and equipped by the Holy Spirit (John 15:16) to fulfill this duty, and there is a harvest field of others who are captive to sin as we were, who need the freedom we are enjoying (Luke 10:2). It does not take a wise man to throw out a lifeline, but simply an open, discerning heart that would seek to shine the spotlight of glory upon the Savior. God does not call the equipped; He equips the called! (1 Corinthians 7:22).

According to 1 Corinthians 7:22 we were called out of slavery to be servants: "For he who was called in the Lord while a slave, is the Lord's freedman; likewise he who was called while free, is Christ's slave." Part of our freedom, then, is in being Christ's servant, and humbly serving others.

45. Spiritual Warfare

We are in a spiritual battle that lasts a lifetime, and we can learn to not only be at war with our sins but to win the battle. "Little children" in the Lord are characterized by their knowledge of forgiveness (1 John 2:12-13), which is the first truth embraced by the soul in repentance. But "young men" in the Lord are characterized by overcoming the evil one through the Word of God living in them (1 John 2:14). Spiritual warfare is more than rebuking the devil, more than praying through our houses and praying against evil spirits. It is maturing in Christ and learning how to apply the principles of Scripture so as to actually win battles by God's grace.

> "He shall say to them, 'Hear, O Israel, you are approaching the battle against your enemies today. Do not be fainthearted. Do not be afraid, or panic, or tremble before them, for the LORD your God is the one who goes with you, to fight for you against your enemies, to save you'" (Deuteronomy 20:3-4).

46. Overcoming Temptation

We who have been involved in P and M have become greatly weakened in character. We have strived to be victorious in our own strength and have failed so often that many of us have given up hope of ever overcoming. But we can overcome temptation, or take the way out, or escape it altogether. Initially, as we are granted repentance from the Lord we must radically amputate all sources of temptation (Matthew 5:29-30), making it physically impossible to gratify our flesh (Romans 13:14). But as we begin to develop the habit of purity it is possible to begin winning over temptation because of the spiritual principle "purity precedes power" (Acts 19:19-20). While we always need to take heed when standing, lest we fall, it is also normal and natural for the maturing Christian to overcome temptation.

One of the greatest ways to overcome temptation is through the Word of God. The freed captive must learn to cherish God's Word in His heart (Psalm 119:11), to meditate on it throughout the day (Psalm 1), and to be empowered by it in times of temptation (Luke 4: 4, 8, 12). "Thy word I have treasured in my heart, that I may not sin against Thee" (Psalm 119:11).

47. Fleeing and Pursuing

One habit that must be developed early in the pursuit of freedom is fleeing and pursuing. "But flee from these things, you man of God, and pursue righteousness, godliness, faith, love, perseverance and gentleness" (1 Timothy 6:11). "Now flee from youthful lusts and pursue righteousness, faith, love and peace, with those who call on the Lord from a pure heart" (2 Timothy 2:22).

This instruction from Scripture is very practical for the one desiring to escape from the trap of impurity. It provides us with the right thing to do when we get hit by a surprise temptation: flee from it and pursue God. Just as the automatic response when putting our finger in the flame of a candle is to withdraw it quickly, so it can become automatic for temptation to trigger us to run from it and run to God.

> "Now it happened one day that he went into the house to do his work, and none of the men of the household was there inside. She caught him by his garment, saying, "Lie with me!" And he left his garment in her hand and fled, and went outside" (Genesis 39:11-12).

48. Vigilance

When we implement radical amputation, radical appropriation, and radical accountability, we do indeed get free from habitual sin. But because we have weak flesh, a strong enemy and the allurements of the world, we must maintain vigilance in order to not fall back into sin. Scripture admonishes us to press on to receive our full reward: "Watch yourselves, that you might lose what we have accomplished, but that you may receive a full reward" (2 John 1:8).

> "But we prayed to our God, and because of them we set up a guard against them day and night" (Nehemiah 4:9).

> "Therefore let him who thinks he stands take heed lest he fall" (I Corinthians 10:12).

49. Victory in Christ

The Christian should expect to be victorious over the world, the flesh and the devil. This is not to say that we will ever be sinless in this lifetime, but we should be living in victory over habitual sin. Whereas living under the authority of sin is normal and natural for the unbeliever, the Christian is assured victory by God's grace (Colossians 1:13).

> "For the law of the Spirit of life in Christ Jesus has set you free from the law of sin and of death" (Romans 8:2), "So then, brethren, we are under obligation, not to the flesh, to live according to the flesh..." (Romans 8:12). "But in all these things we overwhelmingly conquer through Him who loved us" (Romans 8:37),
> "But thanks be to God, who gives us the victory through our Lord Jesus Christ" (I Corinthians 15:57).

50. Live for the Glory of God

The Christian's motive should be to glorify God in all things (1 Corinthians 10:31). The importance of this, as it regards overcoming habitual sin, cannot be overstated. The reason this motive is so important is because God does all things for His own glory (Revelation 4:11; Proverbs 16:4; Romans 9:6; Romans 11:36; Isaiah 45:5-6), and if our motive is to glorify Him we are working in concert with Him to accomplish this same purpose. When we live in pride and seek to lift ourselves up we are at cross purposes with God, and our plans fail. In repentance we turn from exalting ourselves to instead honoring the Lord and our motives are changed to glorify God in all that we do. This brings all the assistance of heaven to our side and God rushes in to help us in our efforts by grace to honor Him. This is a sure guide out of sin. Ask the Lord to change your motives so that all you do brings Him glory and honor.

"Whether then, you eat or drink, or whatever you do, do all to the glory of God" (1 Corinthians 10:31).

"Not to us, O LORD, not to us, but to Thy name give glory, because of Thy lovingkindness, because of Thy truth" (Psalm 115:1).

The
Solution
for the
Spouse

The Solution For the Spouse

51. Refrain from and/or Repent of any Bitterness

The spouse of one who has been involved in impurity has been betrayed and dishonored. If we partake in sexual sins we bring impurity into the marriage and defile the marriage bed, and our spouses are hurt and angered. However, there is an importance for the spouse to not become bitter, be unwilling to forgive, or attempt to assume control of the marriage. An impure person and a bitter, unforgiving, and/or controlling spouse are a recipe for marital disaster.

Whether or not the husband ever repents, the spouse must not allow bitterness to grow in the heart, for if that happens there will be additional defilement spread to all. "See to it that no one comes short of the grace of God; that no root of bitterness springing up causes trouble, and by it many be defiled" (Hebrews 12:15).

Bitterness, like sexual impurity, is defiling, and in order for a couple to make it out of the trap of sin it is important that the husband repent of impurity and the wife remain free of or repent of any bitterness.

> "Let all bitterness and wrath and anger and clamor and slander be put away from you, along with all malice. Be kind to one another, tender-hearted, forgiving each other, just as God in Christ also has forgiven you" (Ephesians 4:31-32).

52. Forgiveness of Spouse

Most men who have lived in impurity have asked for forgiveness many times, only to return to their sin and wound their spouse yet again. Most spouses are tired of granting forgiveness over and over. The granting of forgiveness at times can appear to let the spouse off the hook and so it is often a challenge for the spouse. It requires the grace of God in the heart in order to truly forgive.

Forgiveness is multi-faceted. It is both vertical and horizontal. We must always forgive, in our hearts, before the Lord, for any sin anyone has ever committed against us, so that bitterness does not grow in the heart. This is vertical forgiveness and is illustrated by Jesus' words on the cross, "Father, forgive them for they do not know what they are doing" (Luke 23:34). But horizontal forgiveness should only be granted when the offending party confesses sin and asks for forgiveness. "Be on your guard! If your brother sins, rebuke him; and if he repents, forgive him. And if he sins against you seven times a day, and returns to you seven times, saying, 'I repent,' forgive him" (Luke 17:3-4).

Forgiveness does not equate to trust. Trust must be slowly restored over time, whereas forgiveness must be granted immediately upon request. Horizontal forgiveness means these three things:

- that you promise to not bring this sin up to your spouse again (Psalm 103:10).
- that you will not bring this sin up with other people (Psalm 103:12).
- that you will not dwell on this sin yourself (Jeremiah 31:34).

We are commanded to forgive as God has forgiven us (Ephesians 4:32). The way we treat those who sin against us will be how God treats us. "For if you forgive men for their transgressions, your heavenly Father will also forgive you. But if you do not forgive men, then your Father will not forgive your transgressions" (Matthew 6:14-15).

53. Work as a Team

Marriages that make it out of the trap of sexual impurity are those that work as a team against the sin. It should not be the wife angry at the husband and the husband angry at the wife, but both players on the team angry at the sin and setting out to eradicate it from the life. "For our struggle is not against flesh and blood, but against the rulers, against the powers, against the world forces of this darkness, against the spiritual forces of wickedness in the heavenly places" (Ephesians 6:12).

Oftentimes the man who is coming out of sin is made to feel that he must do certain things before his wife will respect and love him. This is a wrong attitude on the part of the spouse. A man should not withhold love from his wife if she sins against him, neither should a wife require certain steps from her husband before she will obey God to respect, love and submit to her husband.

There must be a team effort, both people joining together to do what each can do to defeat sin and the devil in their marriage.

> "Two are better than one because they have a good return for their labor. For if either of them falls, the one will lift up his companion. But woe to the one who falls when there is not another to lift him up. Furthermore, if two lie down together they keep warm, but how can one be warm alone? And if one can overpower him who is alone, two can resist him. A cord of three strands is not quickly torn apart" (Ecclesiastes 4:9-12).

54. Be an Accountability Partner

The spouse should be willing to get involved in the life of her husband, and at times this means being his accountability partner in the area of purity. She should be willing to work with him to ensure his purity in areas such as computer usage, television and/or movie viewing. She can also help him be accountable for where his "pocket money" is spent. In marriage, two become one, and both lives should be an open book to the other. She should gently and kindly ask hard questions such as, "Have you committed any sexual impurity today? Have you masturbated today? Have you sought the Lord today?" A husband truly repenting of impurity should desire the help of his wife to be free from this debilitating sin and should not object to her checking up on him in any area.

> "For this reason a man shall leave his father and mother and shall cleave to his wife, and the two shall become one flesh." (Ephesians 5:31).

55. Support in Prayer

One of the greatest ministries a wife has to her husband is to pray for him. Often a wife must live with an ungodly husband because he chooses to live with her (1 Corinthians 7:12), and she is called to live a reverent and quiet life before him in the hopes of winning him to the Lord (1 Peter 3:1-6). In such cases she has a powerful weapon against the impurity with which he is intoxicating himself, and that is prayer. In situations where the wife is living with an unbeliever who is not open to rebuke, the wife must learn to "duck" (get out of the way, become quiet, not verbally requiring steps of repentance) and allow God to discipline the impure man (Hebrews 13:4). In such cases she can assail him with fervent prayer (James 5:16).

56. Meet Physical Needs

When a husband has defiled his marriage bed it can be extremely difficult for a spouse to be intimate again. Yet, Scripture requires sexual intimacy in marriage, and warns against denying it.

> "Let the husband fulfill his duty to his wife, and likewise also the wife to her husband. The wife does not have authority over her own body, but the husband does; and likewise also the husband does not have authority over his own body, but the wife does. Stop depriving one another, except by agreement for a time, so that you may devote yourselves to prayer, and come together again lest Satan tempt you because of your lack of self-control" (I Corinthians 7:3-5).

Many times the devil plants seeds of thought such as "Our situation is so unique that we couldn't possibly have sex again." Yet the married couple needs to come to the understanding that denying sex, except for the reasons stated above (a limited time of seeking the Lord, that is mutually agreed upon), is a sin against God. Denying sex invites the devil into the marriage (1 Corinthians 7:5).

In cases where there has been physical adultery committed the offended spouse has the option of divorce, as the unity of the marriage has been broken (Matthew 5:32) and in divorcing she may separate sexually from her husband because he has broken the marriage.

Now, the viewing of pornography, while it is heart adultery, does not carry with it the same option of divorce even as committing heart murder (hating someone) does not carry with it the same consequences as does physical murder.

It is acceptable to divorce where there has been physical adultery committed (though it may not be the best option), but it is not right according to Scripture for the spouse to deny sex if the decision is made to remain married. However, if the man has been physically unfaithful and there may now be a risk that he has a sexually transmitted disease, it becomes important that any sexual activity within the marriage be done with the utmost importance being placed on the physical protection of his wife.

57. Get Godly Counsel

There is much information being disseminated about how to live with and/or help a spouse who is in bondage to P and M; everything from taking a 90-day break from sex to taking over leadership in the home until he repents, and everything in between. We are wise to seek out counsel that conforms to the Word of God, and to reject all counsel that is ungodly even though it might be appealing to us at the moment (Psalm 1:1). "A wise man will hear and increase in learning, and a man of understanding will acquire wise counsel" (Proverbs 1:5). The way of a fool is right in his own eyes, but a wise man is he who listens to counsel.

The local church should be the first place a spouse goes when seeking help and godly counsel. The pastor and elders of the church are not only those who should provide godly counsel, but are also the spiritual authority over us (Hebrews 13:17), and should be able to help. But if further counsel is needed we at Setting Captives Free deal with these issues daily. Our Mentors have also been through training and have much practical experience. Finally, we recommend the National Association of Nouthetic Counselors which can be found online at www.nanc.org or contacted by phone at (317) 337-9100.

58. Honor, Respect and Submit

The wife is called to honor, respect and submit to her husband, which is extremely difficult to do if the husband has lived in a manner that is disrespectful and dishonoring to the Lord, their marriage and the home. Yet honoring and submitting to her husband has more to do with her own relationship with the Lord than anything else. A wife who is in right relationship with the Lord will be enabled by God's grace to honor her husband with her life and her words and to submit to his leadership except unto sin.

> "In the same way, you wives, be submissive to your
> own husbands so that even if any of them are disobe-
> dient to the word, they may be won without a word
> by the behavior of their wives, as they observe your
> chaste and respectful behavior. And let not y'
> our adornment be merely external–braiding the hair,

and wearing gold jewelry, or putting on dresses; but let it be the hidden person of the heart, with the imperishable quality of a gentle and quiet spirit, which is precious in the sight of God. For in this way in former times the holy women also, who hoped in God, used to adorn themselves, being submissive to their own husbands; thus Sarah obeyed Abraham, calling him lord, and you have become her children if you do what is right without being frightened by any fear" (I Peter 3:1-6).

The husband must love his wife even if she fails to respect him, and the wife must respect and submit to her husband even if he fails to love her. "Nevertheless, let each individual among you also love his own wife even as himself, and let the wife see to it that she respect her husband" (Ephesians 5:33).

59. Keep Up Appearance

Many wives, feeling that they could never match the air-brushed glossy porn models their husbands have become intoxicated by might decide to let themselves go as a way to "get even" with their husbands. Other wives have maintained their appearance but their husbands have remained in bondage anyway, so they feel hopeless of ever seeing change come into their marriage.

Both of the above should recognize that honoring the Lord with their bodies should mainly be motivated by a desire to please the Lord. Self control with our bodies glorifies God, and this alone should motivate wives to posses their bodies in self-control.

> "For this is the will of God, your sanctification; that is, that you abstain from sexual immorality; that each of you know how to possess his own vessel in sanctification and honor, not in lustful passion, like the Gentiles who do not know God" (I Thessalonians 4:3-5).

60. Be Willing to Pursue Biblical Steps of Confrontation

Jesus outlined steps to take when someone sins against us, so that we are not without resources to deal with problems. Here are the steps according to Matthew 18:15-17:

> "If your brother sins, go and reprove him in private; if he listens to you, you have won your brother. But if he does not listen to you, take one or two more with you, so that BY THE MOUTH OF TWO OR THREE WITNESSES EVERY FACT MAY BE CONFIRMED. If he refuses to listen to them, tell it to the church; and if he refuses to listen even to the church, let him be to you as a Gentile and a tax collector."

To be clear, the steps are:
1. Private confrontation of spouse (presenting evidence of impurity and calling for repentance).

If spouse does not repent when confronted:
2. Public confrontation of spouse (presenting evidence of impurity to your pastor and elders and asking for help).

If spouse does not repent when confronted:
3. Church discipline: removing the spouse from church (to be initiated by pastors and elders).

It is quite common to hear a spouse say something like, "I have done everything there is to do and yet my spouse continues on in sin." When asked what their pastor and elders have done to help they come up with many reasons why they could not approach church leadership for help. We must not abandon God's method of confronting sin just because it is not convenient or easy. A person who truly wants to help their spouse break free from bondage will follow Jesus' teaching all the way, each step. His way is effective and we can trust Him.

The
Solution
for
Church
Leadership

The Solution for Church Leadership

61. Pastor Should Preach on the Subject of Purity

Gone are the days when we could ignore the subject of P and M and immorality, commonly referred to as PMI. A church that refuses to deal with this subject will find that they are helping to promote ungodly counseling, as they send their sheep off to the world to find help because they themselves lack answers. Pastors must not only be pure vessels themselves (2 Timothy 2:21) but must preach authoritatively on the subject of purity, and issue calls to repentance for those who are in bondage.

Some churches have latched onto Ephesians 5:11-12 and have not continued on to verse 13:

> "Do not participate in the unfruitful deeds of darkness, but instead even expose them; for it is disgraceful even to speak of the things which are done by them in secret. (v13) But all things become visible when they are exposed by the light, for everything that becomes visible is light.

A pastor that begins to proclaim freedom for captives of impurity will no doubt be contacted privately by some in their congregation (both men and women) asking for help. For the pastor who will make himself knowledgeable about how to actually help, this presents excellent opportunities to snatch sheep away from the wolf that seeks their destruction. Much good fruit can come to the pastor, and the church, that will take purity seriously and mount an aggressive and sustained attack against the demonic influences of PMI.

Setting Captives Free has much information (Word documents, Power Point Presentations, books and manuals) for pastors to use in developing a preaching strategy against impurity. Our material is purposefully biblical. Feel free to contact us at any time.

62. Deal With The Captive in a Gentle, Humble, and Firm Manner

Galatians 6:1-3 presents the approach that should be used when working with those involved in impurity:

> "Brethren, even if a man is caught in any trespass, you who are spiritual, restore such a one in a spirit of gentleness; each one looking to yourself, lest you too be tempted. Bear one another's burdens, and thus fulfill the law of Christ. For if anyone thinks he is something when he is nothing, he deceives himself."

This passage indicates the need for those who are spiritual to approach the captive gently and humbly. Harshness and pride to a captive is that which will cause him to turn from you. The minister who will purposely "smell like a sheep" by walking with his people will be much more effective than the one who proclaims like a pontiff from an Ivory Tower.

This identifying with the captive in gentleness and humility should not eclipse the need to be lovingly firm, to require one hundred percent compliance and to take more severe measures when needed (Hebrews 13:17).

63. Use the Word of God to Teach, Rebuke, Correct, and Train in Righteousness

2 Timothy 3:16-17 gives the four-fold purpose of God's Word: "All Scripture is inspired by God and profitable for teaching, for reproof, for correction, for training in righteousness; that the man of God may be adequate, equipped for every good work."

Often a captive will sit under the teaching of God's Word, learn and agree with everything that is taught, only to become puffed up with pride as he gains knowledge. What he needs is to be lovingly rebuked (stop doing this) and corrected (start doing this) and trained in righteousness. The pastor that only uses God's Word to teach is not using three-fourths of its power.

Many times one who is in bondage will truly repent when a pastor issues a gentle, authoritative rebuke. Other times a rebuke combined with correction and training is needed. Freedom is often the result of using God's Word in this manner in the life of captives.

64. Insist Upon Radical Amputation

Teaching about how to overcome temptation when faced with it is useless to one who is a captive. Initial instruction to help free a captive should begin with teaching on God's grace and the need to radically amputate all avenues of sin (Matthew 5:29-30). This radical amputation always requires creativity since each situation is different, but ultimately if there is an avenue left for the captive to gratify his lusts he will take it. Total amputation, radical amputation, is a requirement to freedom.

Purity precedes power (Joshua 7; Acts 19:19-20). Once a captive will become active in plucking out and cutting off all sources of sin, and begin truly seeking the Lord, he will discover that over time his habit of purity produces spiritual power in his life. He will come to the place where temptation no longer has the power over him that it once had, and he can begin, slowly, to go back to a less war-like stance against impurity, being careful to guard his heart and watch himself when standing lest he fall. The move toward a less radical stance should come with much accountability.

The church leadership's initial requirement of radical amputation should be completely followed by the captive, with no objections whatsoever. If there is a waffling on this issue there will be no freedom from captivity. Help the captive to see that his excuses do not matter and will not be tolerated and that he must relinquish his own understanding on these matters (Proverbs 3:5).

65. Teach About Radical Appropriation

Church leaders need to help the captive learn how to appropriate Christ. The one in bondage may have much head knowledge but he is lacking in application and appropriation (Isaiah 44:20). He needs to understand that growing in Christ is about applying God's Word, doing the truth, living out the principles of Scripture (Psalm 111:10) rather than mere reading, learning, memorizing Scripture (as helpful as these things are). Information is not the same thing as transformation.

If the one seeking freedom has followed instructions to radically amputate he now must replace all the time, energy and effort he used to spend pursuing his idol. If he does not seek the Lord he exposes himself to the evil one and his condition will soon be worse off than it was (Luke 11: 24-26).

"Jesus therefore said to them, 'Truly, truly, I say to you, unless you eat the flesh of the Son of Man and drink His blood, you have no life in yourselves. He who eats My flesh and drinks My blood has eternal life, and I will raise him up on the last day. For My flesh is true food, and My blood is true drink. He who eats My flesh and drinks My blood abides in Me, and I in him. As the living Father sent Me, and I live because of the Father, so he who eats Me, he also will live because of Me'" (John 6:53-57).

66. Set Up Daily Accountability

Because the captive was involved in his sin daily, when he comes to his senses he will agree to the need for daily accountability (Hebrews 3:13). Here is where the leadership of the church can utilize lay people in ministry, by setting up accountability partners who can help the captive daily by receiving accountability reports. Leadership should assign the one desiring freedom to 3 or 4 trustworthy men, and set up a plan whereby the freedom seeker contacts one each day of the week for reporting purposes. These do not need to be long discussions, just the statements that he has been free from PMI and has spent time seeking the Lord. The accountability partners can then provide weekly reports to the church leadership.

67. Monitor Progress at Periodic Intervals

There needs to be period monitoring and reporting of the condition of the one desiring to be free from impurity. This monitoring and reporting could be combined with weekly counseling from the pastor/counselor. Questions to ask include, but should not be limited to:

- How is your heart?
- Are you seeking God for grace? Are you experiencing the grace of God which enables us to say no to ungodliness (Titus 2:11-12).
- Have you avoided PMI entirely this week?
- Are you loving your wife? Have you been intimate this week (1 Corinthians 7:5)?
- Are you seeking to restore relationships to the extent possible?

- Is there anything you need to confess and talk about?

"And the apostles gathered together with Jesus; and they reported to Him all that they had done and taught" (Mark 6:30).

68. Require One Hundred Percent Compliance, Allowing No Excuses

When working with those who have been caught in the devil's trap (2 Timothy 2:25-26) there must be full and complete compliance on the part of the one who wants to be freed. "What must I do to be saved?" should be the attitude. Anything short of this will not free the captive (Jeremiah 7:24). The one trapped by the enemy has become adept at deception (Isaiah 44:20), so there will need to be ways to verify his statements of compliance.

> "If anyone does not obey our instruction in this letter, take special note of that man and do not associate with him, so that he may not be put to shame. And yet do not regard him as an enemy, but admonish him as a brother" (2 Thessalonians 3:14-15).

69. Pursue Church Discipline With Those Who Will Not Listen

One deception a slave to sin will believe is that he is "getting better" when he can go a little longer than normal without gratifying his flesh. But we are not after someone "getting better". We are after freedom. The evil one is happy to let out some slack to his captives for a time, only to pull them back in when they feel they are finally gaining ground. Those who persist in rebellion, failing to heed the instruction of leadership should eventually come under church discipline.

It is important to follow through with all the steps listed earlier in Matthew 18:15-17 with those captives who will not listen and instead choose to press on in their sin.

Notice that the reason for expelling the captive is not for his habitual sin but for refusing to listen. This must mean that the counsel of leadership must be such that if followed it would actually extract the idol from the grip of the one

47

enslaved. If the captive does not get free it shouldn't be because the advice he followed was inadequate, but because he was unwilling to be that radical.

70. Encourage Those Who Repent and Receive Them Fully Into Fellowship

Those who repent and escape the trap of the devil should be received fully into fellowship. Once a man has gone for a full year with no viewing of pornography, no masturbation and no sexual immorality, if he is seeking the Lord, then all can be sure that he is most likely free from the fire of impurity. One year is an arbitrary number based upon experience, and there should still remain weekly accountability for the freed captive.

> "But if any has caused sorrow, he has caused sorrow not to me, but in some degree–in order not to say too much–to all of you. Sufficient for such a one is this punishment which was inflicted by the majority, so that on the contrary you should rather forgive and comfort him, otherwise such a one might be overwhelmed by excessive sorrow. Wherefore I urge you to reaffirm your love for him" (2 Corinthians 2:5-8).

The
Solution
for the
Church

The Solution For the Church

71. Assume Responsibility to Get Involved

When one part of the body suffers the whole body suffers. Though sin may be brought into the church by one member of the body, the whole body needs to be willing to help. When it becomes known that someone in the body has been impure a simple statement like the following will go far toward helping the captive, "Hey Mike, I don't know the details, but I understand there are struggles. I want you to know that I love you and am willing to help in any way I can."

The one trapped in sin does not need to be avoided, or shunned (unless leadership is exercising church discipline) and it would be helpful for many members to evidence love, care, concern and support.

> "Brethren, even if a man is caught in any trespass, you who are spiritual, restore such a one in a spirit of gentleness; each one looking to yourself, so that you too will not be tempted. Bear one another's burdens, and thereby fulfill the law of Christ" (Galatians 6:1-2).

72. Commit to Prayer

The trapped captive needs to repent, but it is important to understand that God must grant him the gift of repentance (2 Timothy 2:25). Since repentance is a gift from God the church must actively seek the Lord on behalf of the one in bondage. The best ministry to the one enslaved will be intercession.

The admonition in James 5 to pray for the sick includes the spiritually sick, as is evidenced by the promise of forgiveness of sins:

> "Is anyone among you sick? Let him call for the elders of the church and let them pray over him, anointing him with oil in the name of the Lord; and the prayer offered in faith will restore the one who is sick, and the Lord will raise him up, and if he has

committed sins, they will be forgiven him. Therefore, confess your sins to one another, and pray for
one another so that you may be healed. The effective
prayer of a righteous man can accomplish much"
(James 5:14-16).

73. Become Familiar With Three Radical A's

It has typically been a problem in the church that one struggling with P and M
could not find help from the church. The typical response has been to tell the
captive to "read the Bible and pray more" which lacks substance for actually
helping him out of sin. It is a superficial cure to the deep wound of the captive.

> "And they have healed the brokenness of My people
> superficially, Saying, 'peace, peace,' But there is no
> peace. Were they ashamed because of the abomina-
> tion they have done? They were not even ashamed at
> all; They did not even know how to blush. Therefore
> they shall fall among those who fall. At the time that
> I punish them, they shall be cast down," says the Lord
> (Jeremiah 6:14-15).

Each person in the church should be familiar with the basics of helping another out of impurity so that the church will be better equipped to face the
future with many captives seeking help.

It is simple to memorize the three "Radical A's" to present to someone in
bondage, and then to seek to help them to apply it. Here are the basics for
helping men and women to freedom from impurity:

Radical Amputation

The manner of being free from sinful lust is to radically amputate every avenue through which it enters, and to be radical in cutting it off at the source:

> "If your right eye makes you stumble, tear it out and
> throw it from you; for it is better for you to lose one
> of the parts of your body, than for your whole body
> to be thrown into hell. If your right hand makes you
> stumble, cut it off and throw it from you; for it is

better for you that one of the parts of your body perish, than for your whole body to go into hell" (Matthew 5:29-30).

Jesus is not teaching here the dismembering of our bodies, rather He is teaching the need to be radical in cutting out those avenues through which sin
enters. In other words, He is saying to make it so that it is practically impossible to view pornography or to gratify our flesh in masturbation. We who
truly want victory will not allow any provision for our flesh, to gratify the
lusts thereof (Romans 13:14), for we recognize that if it is available we might
turn to it in a weak moment.

God the Father dealt with sin in this radical manner. Jesus was "cut off" from
the land of the living after God placed our sins on Him (Isaiah 53:8).

The story of Achan in Joshua 7 teaches that hidden defilement weakens the
ability to fight. Only as the Israelites "radically amputated" Achan and his
entire family did they have victory over their enemies. Purity precedes power.

This does not mean that radical amputation is the entire answer to overcoming sin. It is an important step in the change process, but it is not the whole
process itself. This step can't be overlooked, but it must be accompanied with
ongoing seeking of the Lord and growth in grace if we really want to be free.

If you want to be free consider every avenue through which you have fallen,
and set out to make it so that you have zero access to it in the future. The devil
lies and says that real victory would be to have the way to gratify ourselves
and then to refuse it. There does come a time when this victory can indeed
happen, but initially the way to freedom is through a radical removal of the
source of temptation. "Pluck out the eye, cut off the hand." As we are radical
in amputation we find freedom (Matthew 18:8-9).

Radical Appropriation

If we cut off access to all pornography and refuse to masturbate, we will now
have a void (Luke 11:24-26). We used to turn to pornography and masturbation as a drunkard turns to alcohol: for excitement, stress relief, comfort,
medicating of pain, etc. Now, because of radical amputation this option is not
available and we must learn to replace this previous sinful energy in pursuing
our idolatry with pursuing the Lord (1 Timothy 6:11). We have previously
been "feeding on ashes" (Isaiah 44:20) and our souls are starved for nutrition.

Now, as we cut off all our ability to feed on that which destroys the soul it becomes important to begin learning how to truly feed on Jesus (John 6:50-58).

Radical Accountability

We who have indulged in the sin of impurity have made sure that our lives are private so that nobody will discover our sin, and we have been accountable to no one. Now, when we seek to be free we need to learn how to invite accountability into our lives, as daily encouragement is an antidote to the power of sin: "But encourage one another day after day, as long as it is still called "Today," lest any of you be hardened by the deceitfulness of sin" (Hebrews 3:13).

Accountability does not mean a support group, though accountability can happen there. It means reporting in to someone as to how I am living, how my walk with the Lord is, how my sin struggles are going. As our indulging in sin was daily, so now accountability needs to be daily as well (Hebrews 3:13).

74. Attack the Problem Not the Person

If you discover that someone at your church is involved in impurity, please remember that he or she is not the problem. The problem is sin. Yes, the person has been sinning, but be angry at the sin and help to attack it and not the person themselves. The way to do this is to make sure your own relationship with the Lord is right and that you understand that apart from God's grace you are capable of anything that they have done. Help the captive to understand your anger is against the sin but that you still love and care for him and want to work with him to help him to freedom.

> "For our struggle is not against flesh and blood, but against the rulers, against the powers, against the world forces of this darkness, against the spiritual forces of wickedness in the heavenly places" (Ephesians 6:12).

75. Be Willing to be an Accountability Partner

Another way that the members of the body of Christ can help a captive is to volunteer to be his accountability partner. Just simply let him know you are willing to walk with him away from the fire and to safety in Jesus, and that you will help him by holding him accountable.

The captive should be taught to initiate accountability daily. He should phone, email, or fax his status (free from PMI) daily to those who are his partners. He should be instructed that those who will work with him more than likely have busy lives and they may forget to contact him. This is not a reason to plunge into sin, nor to bemoan how his accountability partner didn't provide good accountability. It is up to the captive to initiate accountability. But sometimes he will forget, and the accountability partner should then make contact. When the accountability partner makes contact he needs to not only solicit for the purity report but also remind the one seeking freedom that he is responsible to initiate contact.

76. Watch Yourself

One of the instructions to those who would help others out of sin is to be careful themselves. When dealing with sin issues one gets exposed to some details. Though initially these details can promote feelings of disgust, they can eventually become lodged in the brain of one helping, which can lead to serious problems and struggles for the helper. Many a counselor has ruined their career by succumbing to temptation as it was presented to them by the counselee. There is a real danger is this, and much caution is needed. One of the ways you can alleviate these types of issues is to request the captive not to expose you to the details of the sin.

One of our female ministry partners wrote the following, "I had not struggled with same sex attraction for seventeen years. Then I met a woman who was in the lifestyle, but who wanted help. At first I thought, 'I should be able to do this. If I'm really free, then being with her won't be a problem. I can help her.' But, I allowed the emotional dependency to grow. I allowed the relationship to be too exclusive. I allowed my desire to rescue and her need to be helped pervert our friendship. I didn't go for help when I began to struggle with my thoughts, and I didn't take steps to run away. I thought I could handle it. Well, I'm so grieved to say that I couldn't. I ended up hurting her, my marriage, our church. Next time I'll know that I can't be so proud as to think that I can't fall. I have to do what everyone has to do in the face of temptation. Run from it."

> "Brethren, even if a man is caught in any trespass,
> you who are spiritual, restore such a one in a spirit
> of gentleness; each one looking to yourself, lest you
> too be tempted" (Galatians 6:1).

77. Provide Support to the Entire Family

A man who has intoxicated himself at the devil's bar of pornography and sexual impurity has brought defilement into his marriage and family. It is not uncommon to see a harshness, a critical spirit, anger, and a pharisaical attitude (requiring others to reach a standard that they, themselves, do not live up to) on the part of the captive (Galatians 6:7-8). Oftentimes the spouse will harbor unforgiveness, bitterness, and resentment. The children are often wounded and bruised by the harshness and critical spirits of both parents. Helping a captive to freedom should be the most important part of the healing process, but not all of it. The family must be ministered to also. Churches that will seek to help the family (the entire household) in these situations will have a thriving ministry in the future, when impurity increases in the media and becomes mainstream.

> "And let us not lose heart in doing good, for in due time we shall reap if we do not grow weary. So then, while we have opportunity, let us do good to all men, and especially to those who are of the household of the faith" (Galatians 6:9-10).

78. Refuse to Gossip

Gossip destroys fellowship and ruins relationships. When it becomes known that someone is involved in impurity it is of utmost importance that there be no gossip. The easiest way to halt gossip is to not partake of it, to walk away from it stating, "Have you asked ____ (person's name being gossiped about) about this?"

People in the church often avoid those who have fallen to impurity, and then gossip about them. But it is interesting to note that gossips are to be avoided: "He who goes about as a slanderer reveals secrets, therefore do not associate with a gossip" (Proverbs 20:19).

79. Follow Leadership

There is much joy in the hearts of Christian leaders when they have the pleasure of working in a congregation that supports them, as we are instructed to do (Hebrews 13:17). Godly leaders will pursue freedom for captives of impurity clear to church discipline, if this is necessary. If need be, the leadership will instruct the church on the necessity to avoid one who is in bondage to impurity, if they evidence an unwillingness to repent.

> "I wrote you in my letter not to associate with immoral people; I did not at all mean with the immoral people of this world, or with the covetous and swindlers, or with idolaters, for then you would have to go out of the world. But actually, I wrote to you not to associate with any so-called brother if he is an immoral person, or covetous, or an idolater, or a reviler, or a drunkard, or a swindler—not even to eat with such a one" (1 Corinthians 5:9-11).

Those involved in the church need to support leadership in this area, for the purpose of restoring the sin-slave to his right mind and in order to help facilitate repentance. The goal of church discipline is always restoration, first to the Lord and then to the family and finally to the church. Sometimes steps need to be taken that might seem extreme, but the church needs to support the leadership in all biblical steps they take to bring restoration.

80. Forgive and Rejoice Over Repentance

One of the greatest things that can happen in the life of one who has sinned is for the church, as a corporate body, to forgive him and rejoice over his repentance. It would mean a lot to the freed captive if upon his first anniversary of freedom the church threw a party of some kind. This does not have to be any reminder of his sin but just a party acknowledging the grace of God and its effectiveness in the life of the ex-captive. Include as many in the church as possible to show love and support.

> "And he got up and came to his father. But while he was still a long way off, his father saw him and felt compassion for him, and ran and embraced him and kissed him. And the son said to him, 'Father, I have sinned against heaven and in your sight; I am no longer worthy to be called your son.' But the father said to his slaves, 'Quickly bring out the best robe and put it on him, and put a ring on his hand and sandals on his feet; and bring the fattened calf, kill it, and let us eat and be merry; for this son of mine

was dead and has come to life again; he was lost and has been found.' And they began to be merry" (Luke 15:20-24).

Summary
and
Conclusion

Summary

81. Impurity is Spreading – Statistics

- 2 million porn websites available
- 500-1000 new porn websites daily
- "Over 30% of sites on the World Wide Web are pornographic."   – *USA Today*, April 8, 1998
- Recently, 37 percent of pastors admitted in a Christianity Today survey that they struggle with Internet pornography.   – *New Man Magazine*, 3-25-02
- Over 600 pastors are currently taking the Setting Captives Free Pure Freedom Course at *settingcaptivesfree.com*
- The church needs to recognize that many men in our congregations have the same problems with porn that many outside the church have..." – James Lambert, <u>Porn in America.</u>
- A recent search for the word "porn" at *www.alltheweb.com* produced 23,427,519 hits and unfortunately new sites are being added every day. These sites are depraved and demonic in nature and many even portray illegal acts such as child pornography and rape pornography.

82. False Solutions

<u>Rubber Band Technique</u>
This technique teaches us to wear a rubber band on our wrist and whenever we are tempted simply snap our wrist with the rubber band. The thought is that we will begin to associate temptation with pain and we will stop. This method fails to recognize that impurity is a heart problem (Matthew 15:18-20) and we cannot change our hearts by snapping our wrists.

Visualizing Police Officer Technique

This method teaches us that whenever we are tempted, we should visualize a police office running up to us with a big red stop sign and hand cuffs, shouting "STOP!" This method fails to recognize that temptation is more powerful than the thought of punishment and sin couldn't care less about consequences.

Trail Mix Technique

This method states that in giving in to temptation time and time again we are lacking self-control. It suggests we take a bag of trail mix and train ourselves to eat only a certain number of the trail mix each day, thereby developing self-control. This gimmick fails to recognize the depth and power of sinful bondage and the necessity of having Jesus Christ save us from sin's power.

Regressive Therapy

This technique is becoming increasingly popular in the church today. In essence it teaches us to look to our past for some reason why we sin. This method fails to recognize that sin is a heart problem (Matthew 15:18-20); it is internal, not historical. While our pasts contribute to the path we are on, our own hearts are responsible for getting us on the path. Our past, our pain and our parents may all "grease the track", but our hearts are the engine that propels us on those tracks.

Highly Emotional Experience

This method teaches us that since our hearts and emotions are involved when temptation comes, we should recall to mind an equally powerful emotional experience (such as the death of a parent or the birth of a child) when we're faced with temptation, so that we might be diverted from sinning. This technique fails to combat sin, which is a spiritual problem, in a spiritual way. Visualization is not repentance.

Hypnosis (reprogramming subconscious)

Reprogramming our subconscious is not enough to keep us from sinning, we need new hearts in order to become free. Only God can give us these new hearts.

> "And I will give them one heart, and put a new spirit within them. And I will take the heart of stone out of their flesh and give them a heart of flesh" (Ezekiel 11:19).

83. Don't Be Deceived

There is a danger when someone is in bondage to impurity that they might be overwhelmingly self- convinced that they are saved. Usually this occurs with those who have much biblical knowledge.

> "Or do you not know that the unrighteous shall not inherit the kingdom of God? Do not be deceived; neither fornicators, nor idolaters, nor adulterers, nor effeminate, nor homosexuals, nor thieves, nor the covetous, nor drunkards, nor revilers, nor swindlers, will inherit the kingdom of God" (1 Corinthians 6:9-10).

It certainly is possible that the sin-captive is indeed saved. But while in bondage to sin the assurance of salvation should be missing, otherwise the one in bondage is presuming upon the grace of God.

Normally these people will speak much of Jesus' work on the cross, and looking only to Him for assurance, not of any works we do. This is because they are unwilling to examine their lives for the fruit of righteousness, so they cling to "look only to Jesus" to assure them of their salvation. There is danger here. Assurance of salvation must come from two sources; what Jesus did FOR us on the cross (1 Corinthians 15:1-4) AND what the Holy Spirit does IN us (2 Peter 1:3-4).

> "Now if we have died with Christ, we believe that we shall also live with Him" (Romans 6:8).

There is reason to question the captive as to the reason for the assurance of his salvation (2 Corinthians 13:5).

> "For this you know with certainty, that no immoral or impure person or covetous man, who is an idolater, has an inheritance in the kingdom of Christ and God" (Ephesians 5:5).

84. Deliverance and Demonic Possession

Some groups teach the need for the sin captive to be "exorcised" and delivered from demonic possession. While we readily acknowledge that demonism is all throughout P and M (compare Colossians 3:5 with 1 Corinthians 10:20) we also know that, for the majority of sin captives, there must be deliverance by God through the application of Scripture to their lives, rather than a once-for-all exorcism.

Deliverance from impurity is always by God, never by any other method. But God can vary the means He uses in the deliverance, and the time He takes to deliver, from one person to the next. Like physical healing where He sometimes heals instantly and other times He heals over time, spiritual healing is variable.

The one captive to sin should always be taken to the Lord, to His Word, and encouraged to seek God. It is important to understand the spiritual condition of the captive, for we cannot instruct him to cast out his flesh, nor crucify a demon. "Seek the Lord while he may be found; call upon him while he is near" (Isaiah 55:6).

> "For He delivered us from the domain of darkness,
> and transferred us to the kingdom of His beloved Son,
> in whom we have redemption, the forgiveness of sins"
> (Colossians 1:13-14).

85. Sexual Abuse and Freedom from Sin

Our culture has done an excellent job of teaching men and women that they do not have to be accountable for their sins. One of the ways it has done this is through the teaching that if we had a less-than-perfect childhood then it is no wonder we are involved in sin. If we were abused then it follows that we will gravitate toward the sin of P and M.

There are all kinds of problems with this teaching. First, there are many people who have been abused as children who grew up seeking the Lord and enjoying Him rather than turning to P and M. Also, there are many people who were never abused who are stuck in the trap of P and M. Secondly, sin is always a problem of the heart (Matthew 15:18-20), regardless of what kind of past people have had. Therefore it is more important to focus on the heart when attempting to help sin slaves find freedom in Jesus. While it is important to be compassionate about childhood abuse it is just as important to not allow the captive to use it as an excuse to continue sinful behavior.

In Jeremiah's day this same teaching (blaming our sinful condition on our parents) was being promoted. The people were quoting a proverb about their fathers eating sour grapes which then set the children's teeth on edge. It was a way of blaming the parents for the sin of the children. Jeremiah put a stop to that with one powerful statement in Jeremiah 31:30:

> "In those days they will not say again, 'The fathers have eaten sour grapes, and the children's teeth are set on edge.' But everyone will die for his own iniquity; each man who eats the sour grapes, his teeth will be set on edge" (Jeremiah 31:29-30).

86. There is Hope

No matter how long a person may have been in bondage there is hope for real freedom. At Setting Captives Free we work with people who have been enslaved for 40, 50, 60, sometimes 70 years, and many of them find freedom through the gospel. When God grants repentance in the heart the inevitable result is freedom, so there is every reason to have hope that, no matter how long the bondage has been, real freedom is possible.

> "As for you also, because of the blood of My covenant with you, I have set your prisoners free from the waterless pit. Return to the stronghold, O prisoners who have the hope; this very day I am declaring that I will restore double to you" (Zechariah 9:11-12).

> "Jesus answered them, 'Truly, truly, I say to you, everyone who commits sin is the slave of sin; and the slave does not remain in the house forever; the son does remain forever. If therefore the Son shall make you free, you shall be free indeed'" (John 8:34-36).

87. Get Serious, Get Free

One who wants to find true freedom from habitual sin must get serious with God. Freedom does not come to the one who simply makes a decision to get free (John 1:13), it comes to the one who is given the gift of repentance (2 Timothy 2:25-26). "So then it does not depend on the man who wills it or the

65

man who runs, but on God who has mercy" (Romans 9:16). This sovereign grace of God leaves us at the mercy of God in order to truly be free, and it takes an earnest pleading with the Lord to find freedom. This is serious business. In order to get free, we must get serious.

> "Draw near to God and He will draw near to you. Cleanse your hands, you sinners; and purify your hearts, you double-minded. Be miserable and mourn and weep; let your laughter be turned into mourning and your joy to gloom. Humble yourselves in the presence of the Lord, and He will exalt you" (James 4:8–10).

88. The Power of the Word

Often God will turn over to depravity one who persists in rebellion (Romans 1:24). When He turns them over to their own lusts they are beyond human help (Psalm 107:12). No friend, no parent, no ministry can assist them to freedom because they have hardened their hearts and stopped up their ears. God may leave them in this condition for an extended amount of time. But should He ever choose to bring them to their senses (2 Timothy 2:25-26) and release them from captivity He will do so through His Word (Psalm 107:20). It will not be through behavioral modification principles, techniques, gimmicks or tips that a sinner finds freedom. The Word of God, empowered and applied by the Holy Spirit, is powerful enough to save and completely release men and women from the iron chains of bondage.

> "Because they had rebelled against the words of God, and spurned the counsel of the Most High. Therefore He humbled their heart with labor; they stumbled and there was none to help. Then they cried out to the LORD in their trouble; He saved them out of their distresses. He brought them out of darkness and the shadow of death and broke their bands apart. Let them give thanks to the LORD for His loving kindness, and for His wonders to the sons of men! For He has shattered gates of bronze and cut bars of iron asunder. Fools, because of their rebellious way, and because of their iniquities, were afflicted. Their soul abhorred all kinds of food, and they drew near to the gates of death. Then they cried out to the LORD in

their trouble; He saved them out of their distresses. *He sent His word and healed them, And delivered them from their destructions"* (Psalm 107:11-20, emphasis mine).

89. The Role of the Holy Spirit

The Holy Spirit convicts of sin, righteousness and judgment (John 16:8), draws the sinner to Jesus Christ, grants him repentance, and then seals him in Christ for eternity. He teaches us all things of God (John 14:26). He also baptizes us into Christ (Acts 1:5) and then empowers us for ministry (Acts 1:8).

The Holy Spirit's role in bringing the sinner to repentance and in enabling him to escape the devil's trap can't be overstated. A man may read the Bible much, but if the Holy Spirit is not applying the truth to His heart, his reading will only succeed in puffing him up with knowledge. The Holy Spirit is given us through obedience (Acts 5:32) so as we obey God to believe on Christ we receive the Holy Spirit, Who is responsible for freeing captives through the application of biblical truth to the heart.

90. God-Centered Theology

Some modern theology is man-centered and has a low view of God, which has the effect of keeping sin captives in their shackles. Helping captives to freedom requires teaching God-centered theology so that those in bondage would begin to fear the Lord, which is the beginning of knowledge (Proverbs 1:7), and would begin to lose their fatal attraction with themselves.

God centered theology exalts the glory of God and humbles the pride of man, two very important elements in freeing captives.

> "Guard your steps as you go to the house of God and draw near to listen rather than to offer the sacrifice of fools; for they do not know they are doing evil. Do not be hasty in word or impulsive in thought to bring up a matter in the presence of God. For God is in heaven and you are on the earth; therefore let your words be few" (Ecclesiastes 5:1-2).

"For from Him and through Him and to Him are all things. To Him be the glory forever. Amen" (Romans 11:36).

"Worthy art Thou, our Lord and our God, to receive glory and honor and power; for Thou didst create all things, and because of Thy will they existed, and were created" (Revelation 4:11).

91. Relationship with Jesus

True freedom from sin is a by-product of enjoying a saving relationship with Jesus Christ. Knowing God, through Jesus Christ, is what breaks the bondage of sin and sets captives free, and there is no true and lasting freedom apart from a living and vital relationship with Christ. Knowing principles of Scripture will not break the bonds of sin, rather it is knowing Christ that frees.

"And this is eternal life, that they may know Thee, the only true God, and Jesus Christ whom Thou hast sent" (John 17:3).

"And then I will declare to them, 'I never knew you; DEPART FROM ME, YOU WHO PRACTICE LAWLESSNESS'"(Matthew 7:23).

92. The Importance of Church Attendance

Church attendance is critical to finding freedom from sin. It takes the working of God to be free from sin, not merely gaining knowledge or learning some new truth. God works through His body, the church (1 Timothy 3:15). Therefore no true and lasting freedom will be found apart from the church of God.

The devil is aware that he must first separate a member from the church (1 Corinthians 5:5) before he can destroy him, just as a wolf first separates a sheep from the flock and then devours it. Regular church attendance in a Bible-teaching church is an absolute requirement for finding and enjoying freedom.

> "Let us hold fast the confession of our hope without wavering, for He who promised is faithful; and let us consider how to stimulate one another to love and good deeds, not forsaking our own assembling together, as is the habit of some, but encouraging one another; and all the more as you see the day drawing near" (Hebrews 10:23-25).

93. Resources

Setting Captives Free recommends several resources, which we are including here. We do not mean this to be an exhaustive list, and if you are aware of resources we can examine for inclusion in this list please let us know.

- Desiring God Ministries. Found at http://www.desiringgod.org. John Piper teaches us how to live God-centered lives, and how to be a Christian Hedonist (one who lives for pleasure in God).
- National Association of Nouthetic Counseling. Found at http://www.nanc.org. This is an association dedicated to Biblical Counseling.
- Pure Life Ministries. Found at http://www.purelifeministries.org. This ministry is dedicated to helping men find freedom from P and M and contains an excellent live-in program for those who need the extra accountability.
- Truth For Life. Found at http://www.truthforlife.org. Allistair Begg teaches the Bible with clarity and relevance.
- Grace To You. Found at http://.www.gty.org. John MacArthur is committed to teaching God's Word.
- Shepherd's Grace Church. Found at http://www.shepherdsgrace.com This is the home church of Setting Captives Free, located in Medina, Ohio. (www.settingcaptivesfree.com)

94. Enjoying God

The Westminster Confession Shorter Catechism states that the chief end of man is to glorify God and enjoy Him forever. John Piper suggests a subtle change that clarifies the method of glorifying God by stating "The Chief End of Man is to glorify God BY Enjoying Him Forever." The pleasures of sin are only for a season (Hebrews 11:25), but the pleasures that are in Jesus Christ are eternal (compare Psalm 16:11 with Hebrews 1:3).

There is no real pleasure of God for the one captivated by sin. Freedom in Jesus is the first step to living a life of reveling in God. Our churches today need to be about the business of helping to free captives for the purpose that they might begin to truly enjoy the Lord, for the rest of their lives and throughout all eternity.

95. Free Indeed

In summary, Jesus Christ promises freedom for all who will come to Him (John 8:36). It was written of Him in the Old Testament that He would "set captives free" (Isaiah 61:1-2) and literally millions of lives have experientially verified the truth of freedom in Jesus. Freedom from impurity is not only possible, it is inevitable for all who come to Jesus Christ to get free. It is the main mission of the Messiah to set captives free.

> "And He came to Nazareth, where He had been brought up; and as was His custom, He entered the synagogue on the Sabbath, and stood up to read. And the book of the prophet Isaiah was handed to Him. And He opened the book and found the place where it was written" (Luke 4:16-17).

> "THE SPIRIT OF THE LORD IS UPON ME, BECAUSE HE ANOINTED ME TO PREACH THE GOSPEL TO THE POOR. HE HAS SENT ME TO PROCLAIM RELEASE TO THE CAPTIVES, AND RECOVERY OF SIGHT TO THE BLIND, TO SET FREE THOSE WHO ARE DOWNTRODDEN, TO PROCLAIM THE FAVORABLE YEAR OF THE LORD." And He closed the book, gave it back to the

attendant and sat down; and the eyes of all in the
synagogue were fixed on Him. And He began to say
to them, "Today this Scripture has been fulfilled in
your hearing" (Luke 4:16-21).

Conclusion

In conclusion, we need to understand that the soul of the church is being
raped today by impurity. P and M is dragging off fathers, husbands, sons, and
torturing them, raping them, plundering them, and leaving them half dead.

All this destruction is happening during a time of unparalleled church growth.
This tells us that people are streaming in the front door through mass evange-
lism and the evil one is dragging them out the back door through impurity.
The church must do something about this! The church must go on the offen-
sive, assail the gates of hell and drag out its captives. Ministries need to be
started that can effectively deal with the problem. Pastors need to gain educa-
tion beyond seminary that specifically equips them to help captives to freedom. Leaders need to wake up to the extent and severity of this problem and
begin to address it, offering help to any and all who wish to be free.

God uses His church, and the church alone has the solution of the gospel to
offer captives of impurity. Though impurity seems to be a huge giant stalking
the land and mocking God's people, and in contrast the church seems to be as
ill-equipped for the battle as a young shepherd boy, we must step forward to
the battle and fight for the lives of our families. Let the church be quite assured that the battle is the Lord's, that He promises victory, and that He will

**"Now to Him who is able to keep you from stumbling and
to make you stand in the presence of His glory, blameless
with great joy; to the only God our Savior through Jesus
Christ our Lord, be glory, majesty, dominion, and authority before all time, now and forever. Amen" (Jude 24-25).**